THE
Paint Your Own
HORSES
HANDBOOK

BY
KITTY HIGGINS

by Kitty Higgins

Produced by becker&mayer!, Ltd.
11010 Northup Way
Bellevue, WA 98004
www.beckermayer.com
If you have questions or comments about this product, send e-mail to infobm@beckermayer.com.

an imprint of
■SCHOLASTIC
www.scholastic.com

Scholastic and Tangerine Press and associated logos are trademarks of Scholastic Inc.

Published by Tangerine Press, an imprint of Scholastic Inc., 557 Broadway, New York, NY 10012

10 9 8 7 6 5 4 3 2 1

ISBN: 0-439-72003-6

Printed, manufactured, and assembled in China.

Edited by Melody Moss
Art direction and design by Scott Westgard
Product photography by Keith Megay
Illustrations by Scott Westgard and J. Max Steinmetz
Panorama Illustration by Chris Lyons
Box Illustration by Roberto Campus
Product development by Chris Tanner
Production management by Katie Stephens
Project management by Beth Lenz
Design assistance by Karen M. Testa and Bryan Sears
Additional text and research by Melody Moss and Don Roff
Special thanks to Keith Megay, Don Roff, Phong Le, Leah Smoot, Karen M. Testa, and Craig Varian for assistance with photos.

Photo Credits:

Page 3: Houlihan (Quarter Horse) owned by Jacqueline Hunt, © Keith Megay. **Pages 4-5**: Shadow Dancer (main Arabian image) owned by Laura Green-Morrell, © Keith Megay; Bo (Arabian face) owned by Tracie Consiglieri, © Keith Megay; Arabian in endurance race and black Arabian courtesy of Ernest and Candy Schrader. **Pages 6-7**: A Stunning Steel (main Thoroughbred image) owned by Tracie Consiglieri, © Keith Megay; jumping Thoroughbred and Thoroughbred mare and foal courtesy of Hilltop Stables; Thoroughbred Horse Racing © Joe McDonald/CORBIS. **Pages 8-9**: Main Standardbred image and Standardbred face © Phong Le; Harness Racer on the Track at the Red Mile © Kevin R. Morris/CORBIS. **Pages 10-11**: Houlihan (main Quarter Horse image) owned by Jacqueline Hunt, © Keith Megay; Quarter Horses racing, Quarter Horses team roping, Quarter Horse barrel racing, and palomino Quarter Horse courtesy of the Gary Aichele family. **Pages 12-13**: Madel (main Mustang mare image) and Isabella (Mustang foal) owned by Tomi Nicholas, © Keith Megay; Wild Horses Running © Royalty-Free/CORBIS; Camargue horse © Kathleen Carter. **Pages 14-15**: Main Appaloosa image © Phong Le; Carla High Eagle and Children © Peter Turnley/CORBIS; saddled Appaloosa courtesy of Don and Sharon Johnson. **Pages 16-17**: All Lipizzanner photos courtesy of White Stallion Productions—www.lipizzaner.com. **Pages 18-19**: Peruvian Paso Horse © Kit Houghton/CORBIS; Mare Standing Over Young Colt © Tim Davis/CORBIS; Riding a Peruvian Paso Horse © Kit Houghton/CORBIS. **Pages 20-21**: Clydesdale Horse and Owner © Yann Arthus-Bertrand/CORBIS; Clydesdale Horses Pull Plow © Roger Wilmshurst, Frank Lane Picture Agency/CORBIS; Belgian horses pulling carriage © Melody Moss. **Pages 22-23**: Banjo (main Shetland Pony image) owned by Abby Hunt, © Keith Megay; Wild Shetland Ponies © Kevin Schafer/CORBIS; half-Shetland/half-Thoroughbred pinto foal and two older Shetland Ponies © Phong Le.

Every effort has been made to correctly attribute all the material reproduced in this book. We will be happy to correct any errors in future editions.

04110

The Paint Your Own Horses Handbook is part of the Paint Your Own Horses kit. Not to be sold separately.

PAINT INGREDIENTS: ACRYLIC POLYMER, PROPYLENE GLYCOL, ZINC OXIDE, POLYVINY ALCOHOL, POLYOXYETHYLENEALKYLETHER, HYDROGEN OXIDE, CI 74160: 3, CI 77891, CI 12315, CI 11741, CARBON

Horse Sense

The beauty, power, and grace of horses have enchanted people for thousands of years. In the following pages, you'll explore 10 popular horse breeds from around the world and learn how to paint your own mare and foal in your choice of colors!

A baby or young horse is a *foal*; a one-year-old horse is called a *yearling*. A female foal is a *filly*; a male foal is a *colt*. An adult male horse is a *stallion*; an adult female horse is a *mare*. A *pony* is a small-sized horse of any age.

Horses are measured in *hands*. A "hand" originally meant the width of four fingers, and now means four inches (10.16 cm). The horse is measured from its withers (between the neck and the back) to the ground.

withers

Horses come in many colors! ***Chestnut or sorrel***: reddish brown with mane and tail of same color or lighter. ***Bay***: reddish brown with black mane, tail, and lower legs. ***Brown***: mixed black and dark brown. ***Black***: no brown color anywhere; very rare. ***Gray***: foals are born dark and gradually turn gray or nearly white with age. ***White***: born white with no dark color anywhere; very rare. ***Roan***: white and brown or black hairs mixed throughout the body; unlike gray, roan horses stay the same color throughout their lives. ***Buckskin or dun***: very light tan with black mane, tail, and lower legs. ***Palomino***: gold with white or off-white mane and tail. ***Pinto or paint***: large spots of white and any other color. ***Appaloosa or spotted***: small spots of white and any other color.

To start painting your horse, turn to page 24 for painting instructions.

The ARABIAN

It is early morning, and the Arabian horse is saddled and ready. She paws with her hoof at the dirt as if to say, "Let's go!" She knows that she will carry her rider over 100 miles (161 km) in one day, over steep terrain in the blazing sun. She is confident that she will win this race, because her breed excels at endurance.

The "Arab" is the purest and oldest of all breeds, and its influence is found throughout the equine world. These horses were originally bred in the deserts of Arabia and have changed little in appearance over the centuries. They are known for their courage and speed, and they were often ridden into battle. The Arabian has no equal in stamina for long-distance, cross-country endurance races, and its playful and affectionate personality make it an ideal family horse.

This Arabian is **gray**. Even though it appears white, its skin is black and its coat gradually lightens with age.

Arabians...

- Stand between 14.1 and 15.2 hands high.

- Have beautiful, delicate heads with a **concave** (dished) profile, large eyes set low and wide apart, small ears, and a gracefully curved neck.

- Have short, straight backs, with fewer vertebrae than most other breeds. The tails are set high and are often held up during movement.

The skin of an Arabian's muzzle is unusually soft, and its mane and tail are fine and silky.

Walter Farley's ***Black Stallion*** novels and films are about an Arabian horse.

Arabians are **gray, chestnut, bay, brown, black,** or **roan**. White markings on the face and legs are common.

The THOROUGHBRED

The Thoroughbred's withers flutter as the rider mounts. The horse sees the jumping course ahead and knows what is expected. The rider has trained with this horse for years; they are like one when they move out onto the course. They go forward, first at a trot and then into a full gallop. The horse does not see the judges and crowds that watch in silence as he takes off. In one graceful move, the horse and rider are airborne.

The Thoroughbred was originally bred in Great Britain from Arabian stallions and domestic mares. One of the many reasons for the Thoroughbred's popularity is its speed and endurance, for which it has been bred for over 300 years. The Thoroughbred is the breed most often used in horse racing and is said to be the fastest horse breed on the planet. Thoroughbreds are also a popular choice for many other sports, including hunting, jumping, and polo.

This Thoroughbred is a **bay**. It has a reddish-brown body with black mane, tail, and lower legs.

Thoroughbreds...

- Stand between 15 and 17 hands high.
- Have long, narrow heads with large, widely set eyes.
- Are lean but powerfully built, with long legs and bodies.

Thoroughbreds all share the same birthday—January 1 in the northern hemisphere—regardless of when they were born. A foal born in April would be considered a yearling and would be in training.

An average Thoroughbred can run one mile (1.6 km) in a minute and a half.

Thoroughbreds are **bay, chestnut, brown, black,** or **gray; roans** are rare.

The STANDARDBRED

There is a hush in the crowd as the Standardbred jostles for position at the starting line. He pulls a sulky behind him, with the driver lightly mounted. The harness lies smoothly on the horse's flanks; the sound of leather and metal seem to add to the excitement. "And they're off!" the announcer yells, and the crowd roars. The pace is smooth and the horse's head and neck are arched, his mane flowing in the wind.

The term "Standardbred" originated in the late 19th century, and refers to the "standard" speed that is required for the breed registry. The Standardbred's bloodline came in part from an English Thoroughbred stallion, but the breed was developed in America. The Standardbred is now used primarily in harness racing, and is the fastest harness racer in the world.

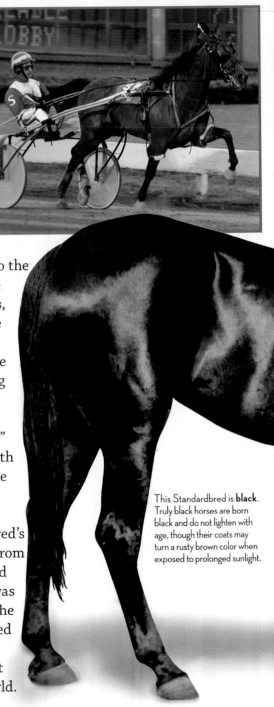

This Standardbred is **black**. Truly black horses are born black and do not lighten with age, though their coats may turn a rusty brown color when exposed to prolonged sunlight.

Harness-racing horses are either **trotters** or **pacers**.

In a *trot*, the legs move *diagonally*: The right front and left hind strike the ground at the same time, then the left front and right hind.

In a *pace*, the legs move *laterally*: The left front and left hind strike the ground at the same time, then the right front and right hind.

Standardbreds...

- Stand 15.2 hands high on average.
- Have deep, thick necks and muscular, straight legs with powerful hindquarters, allowing the horse to reach speeds of 30 mph (48 kmph) or faster.

Standardbreds have large foreheads and nostrils, small muzzles, and generally a more robust head than Thoroughbreds.

Standardbreds are most commonly **brown** or **bay**, but **chestnut**, **black**, and **gray** are also found. Standardbreds rarely have spots or patches.

The QUARTER HORSE

In a small, fenced stall not much bigger than herself, the Quarter Horse stands, saddled with a lasso looped around the horn. The rider mounts from above the corral and they are wedged in together, waiting for the

gate to open. The horse knows this routine well. She is teamed with another horse and rider. They will move as if in a ballet, to help the riders rope the steer. When the moment is right, one of the riders will dismount to pull the steer down. When the horses lean back and pull the ropes tight, the steer will go down.

The Quarter Horse was one of the first breeds of horses developed in the United States. If you have ever seen a rodeo or a working ranch, you have probably seen a Quarter Horse in action. This breed is well known for its "cow sense" and is easily trained to do any job on the ranch.

This Quarter Horse is **brown**. It has a mixed dark brown and black body, with a mane and tail of the same color. It has two white markings: a **stripe** on its face and a **sock** on its right hind leg.

The Quarter Horse was named because of its speed in running a quarter mile (.4 km).

Quarter Horses...

- Stand 14 to 16 hands high.
- Have short, wide heads with widely set eyes.
- Are stocky and broad-chested, with well-muscled hindquarters and a compact body.

Quarter Horses are popular in all equine sports that require a short burst of speed and the ability to turn sharply and quickly.

Palominos can be found among Quarter Horses and other breeds. Palominos have golden bodies with light manes and tails.

Quarter Horses come in many colors: **chestnut, bay, brown, black, gray, roan, buckskin,** or **palomino.**

The MUSTANG

The Mustangs have been driven from the freedom of the open range to a corral that holds them against their will. They do not know that their capture is meant to save them, that they have damaged the cattle-grazing pastures and that the ranchers want them off their land. The corral is a prison to the Mustangs; they run in circles, whinnying into the night. They press against the fence, leaning with all of their weight, and the fence goes down. Free again, the herd steals into the night, knowing that the morning sun will find the horses breathing the air of freedom. The Mustangs do not want to be tamed.

The Spanish brought horses to the New World in the 1500s. In America, they often escaped or were set free. Over the years, Native Americans recaptured and tamed the Mustangs. These horses were often crossed with other breeds.

This Mustang is a **buckskin**, with a light tan body and black mane, tail, and lower legs. Her mane and tail are "snow capped" with white streaks. Some buckskin horses have dark stripes running down their backs; they are know as **duns**.

Mustangs come in all colors: **chestnut, bay, buckskin, dun, brown, black, gray, white, palomino, pinto,** and **spotted.**

Wild horses can be found throughout the world. In the marshes of southern France, Camargue horses allow birds to perch on their backs and catch insects.

Mustangs...

- Tend to be relatively small, averaging about 14.2 hands high. This is because they have to look for grasses to eat in the wild, which is especially difficult in the winter.

Newborn foals can stand within an hour of birth!

The APPALOOSA

The Appaloosa has a colorful, hand-woven blanket draped across his back. Ceremonial feathers are woven into his mane and tail; this is Chief Joseph's horse. Retreating from the Unites States Calvary in 1877, the chief's Nez Percé (nez-PERSE) tribe has packed the few possessions they can carry on their long and risky quest from Oregon to Canada. Though Chief Joseph once exclaimed, "I will fight no more forever," the Nez Percé people—as well as the Appaloosa—endure today.

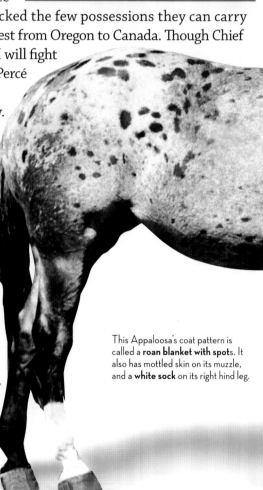

The Appaloosa's history originates with the Nez Percé, who live in what is now the Pacific Northwest region of the United States. The word "Appaloosa" comes from the term "Palouse Horse,"named after a river that runs through Idaho and Washington state. The Nez Percé bred horses to get the strongest, fastest, and most colorful mounts. The strength of the Mustang and the speed of the Quarter Horse give us the Appaloosa that we know today.

This Appaloosa's coat pattern is called a **roan blanket with spots**. It also has mottled skin on its muzzle, and a **white sock** on its right hind leg.

In Quercy, France, cave paintings over 20,000 years old depict spotted horses.

It is estimated that there are 30,000 Appaloosas in Australia.

Appaloosas...

- Range in height from 14.2 to 15.2 hands.

- Have striped hooves, multicolored skin, and a short mane and tail.

- Have coat patterns commonly described in seven terms: solid, blanket, roan, roan blanket, spots, blanket with spots, and roan blanket with spots.

Appaloosas are known as "the horse of many colors." There are so many different patterns of coat color that it is not easy to know what color a foal may be. Most foals are born with a light coat and shed their baby hair. The color is unknown until the shedding is done.

The LIPIZZANER

The Lipizzaner prances around the arena, clearly enjoying himself. The rider removes his hat, and as he bows his head, the horse lifts his left leg and leans forward. His head lowers, almost touching the ground. He and the rider have trained together for 15 years, the horse beginning as a yearling and the rider as a teenager. They know each other very well. There is a mutual respect that draws them together as they perform the "Airs above the Ground," both, for a moment, weightless and then returning to earth.

The Lipizzaner was developed over 400 years to get the breed we know today. It is a combination of many breeds, including the "Spanish Horse," or Andalusian. It is most famous for its dressage moves. Dressage (dre-SAHJ) is a classic form of riding, somewhat like horse ballet. Lipizzaners are also a great breed for driving, jumping, reining, endurance races, vaulting, and of course, for pleasure riding.

This Lipizzaner is **gray**. Truly white horses have pink skin and remain the same color their entire lives; they are very rare.

The Lipizzaner was originally bred by the Spanish Riding School in Vienna, Austria. During World War II, the U.S. Army helped save the breed from extinction.

Lipizzaners...

- Stand 14.3 to 16 hands high.
- Are slow to mature, but can live up to 35 years.
- Are considered rare; there are fewer than 3,000 purebred Lipizzaners in the world.

Lipizzaners are born **black** or **bay** and slowly turn "**white**" (actually **gray**) by the time they are six to ten years of age.

The PERUVIAN PASO

The Peruvian Paso is only hours old, but she gracefully rises to her feet and takes her first steps. As if on tiptoe, she moves with a melodic gait that has been bred through generations. As the hours pass and her confidence builds, the foal glides along the pasture fence with the "tic-a-tic-a" of tiny hooves brushing against the grass. Riders will look to her in the future as a horse that can be ridden comfortably for miles. This horse has one of the smoothest gaits in the world.

A horse's gait refers to the way it moves. Most horses have only three gaits: the walk, the trot, and the canter or gallop, but some horses— like the Peruvian Paso—have other specialized gaits. The Peruvian Paso originated in South America after the first horses were brought to Peru by the Spanish in the 1500s. The result of centuries of breeding in the mountains and plains of Peru, the Peruvian Paso eventually became renowned for its smooth, four-beat, lateral gaits, in which the front legs swing out and the back legs are held low under the body. The gaits are passed on to the Peruvian Paso's offspring, and even a very young foal will naturally perform some of these movements. Other popular "gaited" breeds include the Paso Fino, the Tennessee Walker, the American Saddlebred, the Missouri Fox Trotter, and the Icelandic Horse.

Peruvian Pasos...

- Stand between 14 and 15.2 hands high.
- Have well-proportioned heads, expressive eyes, delicate muzzles, thick necks, and long manes and tails.
- Are compact and muscular with exceptionally strong limbs.

Paso means "step" in Spanish, and the Peruvian Paso is noted for its specialized, smooth gaits. The breed is reported to reach speeds of up to 16 mph (26 kmph) without jostling its rider.

This Peruvian Paso is **gray** with a reddish mane and tail. Its coat is **dappled** with a pattern of round, white spots.

Peruvian Pasos can be found in almost any color, with or without white markings.

The CLYDESDALE

Lumbering along the tilled rows, the Clydesdales— adorned in harnesses and chains—pull the field plow along. Without the help of the strong horses, the farmer could not grow crops that feed hundreds of hungry people. As the plow's blade cuts grooves into the soil, the Clydesdales tug the heavy farming tool across acres of land, tirelessly and without complaint.

The Clydesdale was bred in Scotland. The original name for Lankarshire, Scotland was Clydesdale. The need for animals to work in the fields and farmlands led to this muscular, sturdy breed. Soon, the need for draft horses to pull carts loaded with produce and other food for the population led to the regular use of the Clydesdale as a real multipurpose workhorse. Draft horses were the movers and pullers before the invention of trucks and cranes. The Belgian, Percheron, and Shire are just a few of the other well-known draft breeds.

This Clydesdale is **bay**, with a reddish-brown body and black mane, tail, and lower legs. Its black legs are covered, however, by extensive white markings. Its coat displays a faint **roan** pattern, with mixed white and brown hairs.

A **draft** horse is a large breed of horse that has been adapted for pulling heavy loads in harness. Today, draft horses are popular in parades and as carriage horses for tourists.

Clydesdales...

- Are 16 to 18 hands high and weigh between 1,700 and 2,000 pounds (643-756 kg). Some of the mature stallions are taller and weigh up to 2,200 pounds (832 kg).

Clydesdales are most commonly **bay, brown,** or **black. Roans** and **chestnuts** are also possible. The face and legs are always white; long, silky feathering around the feet is also a trademark.

The SHETLAND PONY

The northern wind of the island howls like a hungry wolf across the green fields. Enveloped in their double-thick winter coats, herds of Shetland Ponies fight against the harsh elements of the Scottish island.

With such a cold climate, the ponies have remained small to conserve their body heat. When the grass of the area turns poor, the sure-footed ponies travel miles—fighting strong winds, steep hills, and jagged rocks in search of their next meal.

The Shetland is the smallest of the British breeds. Originally bred over 2,000 years ago on the Shetland and Orkney Islands off the north coast of Scotland, they have been exported all over the world. In past years, Shetland Ponies were bred to work underground in mines. But they were also good riding and driving ponies, and that is how we best know them today.

This Shetland Pony is a **flaxen chestnut**, with a reddish-brown body and lighter mane and tail. Its coat shows a faint dappling pattern.

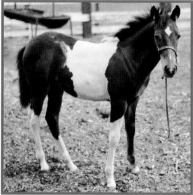

Shetland Ponies...

- Are measured in inches, unlike other horses. They grow to a maximum of 42 inches tall (106.6 cm), measured from the withers.

- Have small heads; deep, stocky bodies; short legs; and small feet. They are very strong for their size.

- Are independent but obedient.

Shetland Ponies are often **pinto** colored, like this half-Shetland/half-Thoroughbred foal. Pintos have large spots of white and any other color.

Shetland Ponies often live long lives. The chestnut pony on the right is 30 years old; the black pony on the left is 10.

Shetland ponies are found in all colors except spotted: ***chestnut, bay, brown, black, gray, dun, roan, palomino,*** and ***pinto.*** They have thick coats and heavy manes and tails.

Painting Instructions

- **IMPORTANT: Read all instructions before you begin to paint!**

- To protect from spills, place newspaper over your work surface and wear old clothing.
- Have a container of water handy for cleaning the paintbrushes between colors and a cloth or paper towel for removing excess water from the paintbrushes.

NOTE: These are water-based acrylic paints. They dry very quickly, and may scratch off. To remove paint from your hands, wash them in warm, soapy water.

General Painting Tips:

- Use the thicker brush for larger areas, and the thinner brush for smaller details.

- Do not let the paints dry on the brushes. Rinse the brushes immediately after using each color. Be sure to change the water when it becomes dirty.

- If the paint is globbing, dip your paintbrush in water to thin the paint.

- You may need to use multiple layers of paint to achieve your desired effect.

- Let each coat of paint dry thoroughly before adding another. The paint should dry within 5-10 minutes.

- To correct a mistake while the paint is still wet, wipe it off with a wet paper towel.

- If you want to mix paints, put each color on a plastic lid or a paper plate before blending them together. Try mixing just a few drops at a time until you reach the desired color. You can add a little white or black paint to get lighter or darker shades of any of the colors. Do not mix the colors in your paint pots!

Paint Chart

The paint comes in numbered pots. In the following instructions we refer to the color-coded paints below:

Black Paint Pot#1	**Brown** Paint Pot#3	**Green** Paint Pot#5
White Paint Pot#2	**Tan** Paint Pot#4	**Red** Paint Pot#6

Horse Painting Hints:

- Paint large areas first. You may find it easier to hold onto the horse's tail or one of its legs while you paint. Avoid touching the wet paint!

- Smooth out any large globs of paint before they dry.

- Use **rapid, feathery brushstrokes** for the best result (as shown). Let the paint dry for 5-10 minutes and then repeat this step until you have a smooth, even color.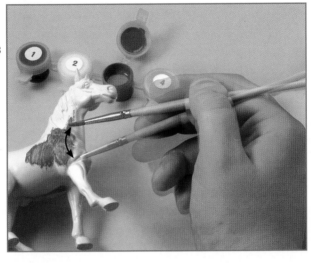

- Use a toothpick **to paint the eyes** or other detailed areas. Dot the color on with just a tiny amount of paint.

- For **Appaloosas** or **pintos**, try using a pencil to outline the spotted areas before you begin painting. This is demonstrated on page 29.

Now you can paint your horses! Review the many colors described in the next section, and decide how you would like to paint your mare and foal.

In a hurry? Try painting the leopard Appaloosa on page 28. It's a snap!

Chestnut

Chestnuts, also known as sorrels, are reddish brown. The mane and tail are the same color as the body, or lighter.

1. Paint the entire body **brown (#3)**, EXCEPT for the mane and tail. Remember to paint in light, feathery strokes. After one coat of this color, let it dry. Your horse should look similar to this after one light coat.

2. Repeat as necessary, up to four coats, allowing the paint to dry for about 5-10 minutes between each coat. After a few coats, your horse should look similar to this one.

STOP! If you want to continue painting a chestnut, you can paint the mane and tail the same **brown (#3)** color. If you want to paint a **bay** instead, move on to the next section.

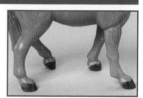

3. Paint the hooves **black (#1)**.

4. Using a toothpick, paint the eyes **black (#1).** See this step on page 25.

5. To paint additional white markings on the face and legs, see page 31.

Bay

Bays are similar to chestnuts, but they have black manes, tails, and lower legs.

1. Continuing after step #2 in the chestnut section above, paint the mane, tail, and lower legs **black (#1)**. Be sure to add an extra coat of black on the lower legs, to cover the brown you've already painted.

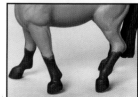

2. Paint the hooves **black (#1)**.

3. Using a toothpick, paint the eyes **black (#1)**. See this step on page 25.

4. To paint additional white markings on the face and legs, see page 31. Your finished bay should look something like this one.

Palomino

Palominos have gold-colored bodies with white or blond manes and tails.

1. Paint the entire body **tan (#4)** using light, feathery strokes. Do not paint the mane and tail. After one coat of this color, let it dry.

2. Repeat as needed, allowing the paint to dry between each coat. Your horse should look similar to the one shown.

3. Using a toothpick, mix a very small amount of **tan (#4)** with a larger amount of **white (#2)**, as shown.

4. Now use the "blond" color you just created to paint the mane and tail.

5. Paint the hooves **black (#1)**.

6. Using a toothpick, paint the eyes **black (#1)**. See this step on page 25.

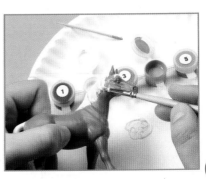

7. To paint additional white markings on the face and legs, see page 31. When you are finished, your palomino should look similar to the one shown.

Appaloosas

Of all the horse colors described in this book, the Appaloosa is the only one that is also a widely recognized breed! Appaloosas have small spots on their bodies, and they display a variety of color patterns. Two of the most common are "leopard" (a white background with colored spots all over) and "spotted blanket" (a colored background with a white blanket over the hips, and colored spots on the blanket area).

Leopard Appaloosa

1. To create a leopard Appaloosa, first choose **black (#1), brown (#3)**, or **tan (#4)** as the color for the spots. Use only one of these colors for your Appaloosa. The one shown here is **brown (#3)**.

2. Dab small amounts of colored paint in spots around the horse's body, using the thicker paintbrush for larger spots and the thinner one for smaller spots. For very small spots, use a toothpick.

3. Paint the ears in the same color as the spots.

4. Paint streaks in the mane and tail, using the same color as the spots.

5. Paint the hooves **black (#1)**.

6. Using a toothpick, paint the eyes **black (#1)**. See this step on page 25.

Spotted Blanket Appaloosa

1. To create a spotted blanket Appaloosa, first choose **black (#1)**, **brown (#3)**, or **tan (#4)** as the color for the background. The one shown here is **black (#1).**

2. Use a pencil to outline a blanket area over the hips.

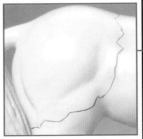

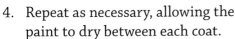

3. Paint the body in the color you have chosen, EXCEPT for the blanket area you outlined and the mane and tail. Remember to paint using light, feathery strokes. After one coat of this color, let it dry.

4. Repeat as necessary, allowing the paint to dry between each coat.

5. Dab small amounts of colored paint in spots around the unpainted blanket area, using the same color as the body. Use the thicker paintbrush for larger spots and the thinner one for smaller spots. See step #2 of the leopard Appaloosa for this technique.

6. Paint the mane, tail, and hooves **black (#1)**.

7. Using a toothpick, paint the eyes **black (#1)**. See this step on page 25.

8. To paint additional white markings on the face and legs, see page 31.

Pintos

Pintos have large white spots mixed with any other color. They are sometimes referred to as paints, and in some parts of the world they are divided into two color types: piebald *(white and black) and* skewbald *(white and any other color except black).*

1. To create a pinto, first choose a background color type, like **chestnut, bay, palomino**, or **black**. The one shown here is **black**.

2. Use a pencil to outline the large areas that you want to remain white. You can follow the example shown here, or you can create whatever pattern you like!

3. Paint the body and tail in the color you have chosen, but leave the blanket area you outlined and the mane unpainted. After one coat of this color, let it dry.

4. Repeat as necessary, allowing the paint to dry between each coat

5. Pintos often have manes and tails of mixed color, and the white in their manes frequently connects to the white spots on their necks. After penciling off the parts of the mane you want to leave white, paint the rest according to the background color you have chosen. See the photo to the left.

6. Paint the hooves **black (#1)**.

7. Using a toothpick, paint the eyes **black (#1)**. See this step on page 25.

8. To paint additional markings on the face and legs, see page 31.

Markings

Add your choice of white markings on the face and legs! Be sure to use multiple coats of *white (#2)* paint, if needed, to cover the colors you've already painted.

Face Markings:

| Star | Stripe | Blaze |

Leg Markings:

Sock
A sock goes about halfway up the horse's lower leg.

Stocking
A stocking goes up to the middle joint of the horse's leg.

The sky is the limit when it comes to the colors you can paint! Feel free to experiment with different color combinations. Use the photos of the different horse breeds in this book as examples.

Painting Your Panorama

Give your horses a change of scenery with these paint-by-number panoramic backgrounds!

- Your panorama has a different scene on each side. If you want to complete both sides, let the paint dry on one side before you start on the next.

Your barn scene should look like this when you are finished painting it.

Your mountain scene should look like this when you are finished painting it.

- Review the "General Painting Tips" on page 24 before you begin.

- Match each numbered space on your panorama with the corresponding numbered color in your paints. Start with a very small amount of paint on your brush.

NOTE: Some areas are white or blue— they are not numbered and you do not need to paint them.

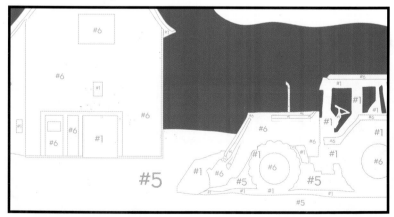

- Paint the smaller areas first, then move on to the larger spaces.

Now set up your panorama behind your horses!